CW00409899

Contents

"This book allows me to
share and expand on
my life lessons further.
Even if it inspires just
one person to take a different
direction or give them courage
to go for something they
have been putting off and
overcome any obstacles or
barriers, that is a great
accomplishment for me"

I want to know if you did something different
after reading this @howigothere2022

Preface

Its 4th February 2022 and my dream cruise with friends, postponed twice due to the Covid 19 pandemic is now finally going ahead. I did not for one minute think this holiday would be my lightbulb moment to share my life experience, but I guess you never know when inspiration is going to strike.

I am very lucky to have had opportunities to explore many destinations around the world and once our friends introduced us to Celebrity cruises, well, we really got the bug. There's something about the variety and choice of activities on the ship, balanced with the chance to just relax and have a pampering day. Exceptional restaurants with the best service from the friendliest crew who can't do enough for you add to the experience. (Oh! I had to fit in a treadmill session on the sea days as my clothes would just not fit by the end of the cruise.) This amazing experience on the Celebrity Apex ship, which I describe as a 'ship of art' was the stunning backdrop to my decision to write this book.

Looking back, I believe that this cruise created for me the perfect environment for the seed of inspiration to take hold. In between spa trips, I gravitated towards a quiet spot in a relaxing, wide chair. This became my tranquil place to watch the sea waves, read or just shut my eyes and take in the smell and sounds of the sea.

There was definitely inspiration in the excitement of dressing up for the evening entertainment in the theatre. You can party till late with some great sounds from the DJ's or just relax with a drink. For almost 2 years we didn't get to dress up and socialise, we had to stay away from crowds, and this felt really special.

The first night in the theatre and the show was Crystalize, breathtakingly mesmerising and I run out of superlatives trying to describe this stunning show. This is where I first set eyes on the Cruise Director Giuseppe Moschella, very entertaining and charming, not least his sparkly black shoes! We were very lucky to get to know him in person. I have never met an individual who goes out of his way to connect with his guests in the way he does, always full of energy with so much generosity and kindness. He radiates happiness.

We attended his motivational seminar about his book, '10 simple ways to find Happiness'. I'm normally skeptical about these types of books, but I was curious and as you know, I had some time on my hands. Having read the book with attending the seminar, well... that was it, I had my lightbulb moment and inspiration to do this for myself.

I'm not a celebrity or a CEO, but everyone has a story to tell. Back in August 2020, my friend and colleague Sarah McKee asked me if I would write a blog for a LinkedIn post, 'How I got here... Being a BAME female in a man's world' and now editor for this book. When you read my story, I hope you will understand why I am proud of my journey – I would never have ever thought for one minute that I would be a Senior Manager in the construction industry, surrounded by talented engineers. I was later told that my blog received the most hits on LinkedIn. And for me personally, so many comments on how inspiring my story was for them.

It is in telling our stories that we learn about our differences, our similarities and how everyone grows in their own way. It is through storytelling that my work life and cruise life come together: while I was on board, I learnt about and got to know many fantastic crew members on the ship and their own journeys and opportunities for being promoted. I just love company cultures where they encourage development and promotion within. They too would relate to my story, and I certainly relate to theirs.

I am so grateful that Giuseppe agreed to be my mentor for this book. Grazie mille, molto apprezzato.

Being a BAME female in a man's world

The Blog post that started it all:

I'm Anita Solanki, 2nd generation Hindu of Indian heritage, born in Leicester, England and now live in a lovely small village in North Leicestershire.

As a young teenage girl, I had great ambition to be something, have my own business and be successful. Coming from a working-class background, would I be the same as my parents or could I break the mould and do something different? My teachers said I had good brains, my mum thought I should be a doctor. So, what do I do? As it turned out, I fell in love at 16, dropped out of university and for 10 years, my career ambitions went on hold as I fulfilled the role of a wife and a mother to two young children.

I was 18 when I got married and all my ambition to be a successful business owner went on hold, as I fell in love with a boy in secondary school and, in line with the strict culture of 33 years ago, we did our honourable duty and married.

For 8 years, I think I forgot who I was - they say love is blind! I lived with my husband's extended family who ran a family business manufacturing jeans. This meant that although I lived in a wonderful home, I became locked in a bubble.

I had my first son at 21 and the second at 24. In between changing nappies, cleaning and cooking, I also became part of the jeans business. I did everything from material supplies, cutting patterns, quality control, sales, invoicing and marketing to cleaning out loos and sweeping up. They were tough days and long hours, but it taught me the end-to-end process of a business.

My life turned around when I took on my first ever real mainstream job with a Midlands water company at the age of 26. I learnt so much, am thankful for all the development opportunities and the promotions supported by some great managers. The first time I became a team leader, managing people, managing high profile projects. I didn't realise I would break so many barriers and go onto chair Regional and National committees. I became a Director of communications and Associate Director for a National trades body.

It felt like time to move on after 17 years at the water company. Great managers, great people, but I had reached the highest I could go in my field and at national level. I spotted an intriguing role with Kier and thought 'I'm in my mid-forties, I have a huge network of highways, utilities, contractors and supply chain in the industry. I'm comfortable. Can I leave it all behind? It's now or never.'

It's 2015 and I find myself travelling all over the UK, Scotland one minute, London, Exeter, Anglian region and so much more. I went on to win 3 awards 3 years in a row for innovation in partnership with supply chain colleagues, which really raised the profile for us in our industry. Where I held myself back, someone believed in me.

By 2018 another opportunity arose within Kier. From my network of contacts, I was approached about a role with Kier Joint Venture EKFB, who had been appointed to deliver 80km of civil engineering on HS2 a high-speed train project, the biggest of its kind in Europe. Infrastructure was a new world and a chance to learn something new, using everything I have learned so far and another award under my belt. So, I'm using my skills of organisation, collaboration, establishing external relationships and creating usable, end-to-end processes to keep our whole team on track and compliant. I feel like I have found my home at EKFB, and I can really be myself. Our inclusivity is a real culture, not just an EDI, Equality Diversion and Inclusion policy that sits on a shelf.

We must continue to challenge ourselves and this book is an exciting opportunity to share my experience further and connect to a larger network.

1. My upbringing

Setting my values

I was very lucky to be brought up in a stable home with hardworking parents.

Both my parents were born in India but my dad at a very young age lost his father at sea on travel to Africa. They had to accept the worse. My grandma married again and they went onto settle in Africa where my dad became part of a bigger family with 3 further brothers and 3 sisters. He then took the bold step of coming to the UK in the late sixties and was able to call the rest of the family over.

My mum and dad had an arranged marriage over a photograph! My mum came over from India in 1968. I was the first grandchild born in Dec 1969 and know I was very much loved by my grandparents', uncles and aunts. I was really spoilt.

My dad was an engineer from a working -class background. He is now retired and is proud to say that he never had a sick day in his life. My mum used to sew at home and work in a plastics factory packing boxes in the evenings so that they balanced looking after me and my siblings between them.

I was the eldest child with a younger sister and brother and yes, like many elder siblings, I was held responsible for their actions. I should know better I'm the eldest! I think that is why I have always needed to prove I am always doing my best... As an older child entering my teens, my head was always buried in my books, I had the neatest handwriting and won best writing competitions. I was very shy growing up and often mistaken as moody, it took me time to trust and make friends.

I did take part in many school activities though, I was in the choir, I had lead roles in plays, I was even chosen to play Mary in the Christmas nativity play as the drama teacher wanted the best voice, (I can't sing as well anymore!) I played netball and rounders and was a great back fielder as I could really lob the ball far.

I went on to play steel drums, the harmonium and started up Indian traditional Kathak dancing. Together with my sister and friends, we took part in local Community performances. In my mid-teens, we took part in our local community traditional folk lore dance competition across the different cities

I went on to play steel drums, the harmonium and started up Indian traditional Kathak dancing. Together with my sister and friends, we took part in local community performances . In my mid-teens, we took part in our local community traditional folk lore dance competition across the different cities, where I had a lead part. The competition was at De Montfort Hall in Leicester, which seemed like the grandest venue I had ever seen. When we won this tremendous competition, it was a huge achievement for us and milestone I still look back on today.

As soon as I was old enough, I took on Saturday jobs wherever I could - mostly in retail. I worked hard and remember busy Christmases in Boots, where I was Chief Cash till person, we didn't stop all day. Or my next job in Dorothy Perkins where I just loved putting outfits together and was promoted to become Chief Cashier.

Lessons learnt:

- Time management
- Coordination
- Planning
- Managing money (more cash in those days)
- I could be trusted
- Customer service

My dad was very strict as I was growing up but the lessons I learnt from my parents that have stuck with me to this day are:

- Honesty in all our dealings
- Hi moral ethics
- Not to be afraid of hard work
- Treat all as you would like to be treated
- Respect your elders

These basic lessons I would say are my inner core values and foundation to what I am today.

If my dad could go through living in 2 different continents and start new beginnings when coming to the UK, well any obstacles I face seem so much smaller.

2. In the beginning

Learning my strength

I was very lucky to be brought up in a stable home with hardworking parents.

Both my parents were born in India but my dad at a very young age lost his father at sea on travel to Africa. They had to accept the worse. My grandma married again and they went onto settle in Africa where my dad became part of a bigger family with 3 further brothers and 3 sisters. He then took the bold step of coming to the UK in the late sixties and was able to call the rest of the family over.

My mum and dad had an arranged marriage over a photograph! My mum came over from India in 1968. I was the first grandchild born in Dec 1969 and know I was very much loved by my grandparents', uncles and aunts. I was really spoilt.

My dad was an engineer from a working -class background. He is now retired and is proud to say that he never had a sick day in his life. My mum used to sew at home and work in a plastics factory packing boxes in the evenings so that they balanced looking after me and my siblings between them.

I was the eldest child with a younger sister and brother and yes, like many elder siblings, I was held responsible for their actions. I should know better I'm the eldest! I think that is why I have always needed to prove I am always doing my best... As an older child entering my teens, my head was always buried in my books, I had the neatest handwriting and won best writing competitions. I was very shy growing up and often mistaken as moody, it took me time to trust and make friends.

I did take part in many school activities though, I was in the choir, I had lead roles in plays, I was even chosen to play Mary in the Christmas nativity play as the drama teacher wanted the best voice, (I can't sing as well anymore!) I played netball and rounders and was a great back fielder as I could really lob the ball far.

I went on to play steel drums, the harmonium and started up Indian traditional Kathak dancing. Together with my sister and friends, we took part in local Community performances. In my mid-teens, we took part in our local community traditional folk lore dance competition across the different cities

I went on to play steel drums, the harmonium and started up Indian traditional Kathak dancing. Together with my sister and friends, we took part in local community performances . In my mid-teens, we took part in our local community traditional folk lore dance competition across the different cities, where I had a lead part. The competition was at De Montfort Hall in Leicester, which seemed like the grandest venue I had ever seen. When we won this tremendous competition, it was a huge achievement for us and milestone I still look back on today.

As soon as I was old enough, I took on Saturday jobs wherever I could - mostly in retail. I worked hard and remember busy Christmases in Boots, where I was Chief Cash till person, we didn't stop all day. Or my next job in Dorothy Perkins where I just loved putting outfits together and was promoted to become Chief Cashier.

Lessons learnt:

Having pride in everything you do no matter how small the task, it's not beneath anyone.

Hard work doesn't kill you, it certainly made me stronger. I don't fear any task making me open to challenges. Even cooking for a party of 50!

It may not seem like it at the time but hard work and what may feel like menial tasks are valuable life skills;

- Planning
- Organisation
- Coordination
- Time management
- Buying
- Selling
- Money management
- Learning an end-to-end processes of a business

You are a vital component to help the world go round. These skills served me well for my later career.

3.

Branching out

Learning to believe in myself first

So I am now 26, and although I qualified as a hairdresser, with 2 kids we needed to get our own place after leaving the extended family. My first main job was in a water company.

On the first day I was early. Arriving at the office was the first few engineers all males! In the end there were 9 male engineers with me as the only female. Having had a sheltered life in the family business bubble for 8 years, this was a shock to the system. Feeling like I may not have the right skill set in the first place my anxiety was rising. I rang my husband, saying "I don't know if I can do this". I think hearing myself say the words made me realise that I was being given an opportunity, I decided right then that being female or BAME would not hold me back from anything. He told me to not to make any rash decisions and just give it a go. I did and it was the best decision of my life as this company took me to heights I could never imagine and stayed for 17 years.

I soon found out I actually had some good skills; I was attentive and organised. I understood instructions well, succeeded at everything asked of me and I soon became in charge of contract administration. My confidence increased and I got used to being the only female and BAME. This role raised my profile where I was invited to attend important meetings and industry events. It was daunting, but also a privilege and an opportunity that I took. Networking turned out to be a key part of my career and a valuable skill.

I got promoted a few times very quickly after I took on a team leader role for a new department looking after Street work legislation. I went on to be the business owner of a major project led by government changes impacting the end-to-end processes. I nearly backed out and started looking for another less responsible job as I didn't think I could deliver something so high profile as it impacted the end-to-end processes of the whole company. My move was blocked, a couple of Senior Managers told me I was the best person for the job. Wait." Somebody pinch me·" Are they talking about me?

I was responsible for interpreting the new rules for the IT project and Exec team to secure project funding. Senior management believed in me when I hadn't believed in myself, but the project was a great success having one of the best compliance performances in our industry. I had many challenges including moving my team of 10 from the Leicester office to the Coventry office as part of my wider management team and to recruit another 40 people in 5 weeks. Yes, a huge set of challenges, but with teamwork and the support of some great colleagues, we did it!

Lessons learnt:

Believe in yourself and get over any doubts.

You have to tackle what is in front of you, grasp, it give it a go don't fear failure.

Don't let your self-confidence get the better of you. Imposter syndrome? Feel like you're not good enough for the job? You are good enough.

You may not be the expert of everything, but you will be surrounded by colleagues that can help you. It's OK to ask for help, it shows a different strength.

I was good at using industry experts to bounce off my ideas, whether we had the same interpretation of certain legislation rules before we made substantial investment.

I always questioned my self-confidence, oldest child having to be good enough syndrome. Until someone says you are not doing great you are doing great!

Moving up

Learning to invest in myself

I started as an agency member for 4 years in the water company doing contract admin tasks, copying paper plans, taking minutes, arranging meetings. The consultants I looked after were doing vital surveys to promote major water mains schemes by the Drinking Water Inspectorate. This was high profile and managing the contracts got me noticed. I managed to get into Network management and scheduling for field operatives as my first directly employed job with them.

I began to feel that my lack of qualifications was holding me back. So even though I was 30, had a fulltime job and two kids under nine, I decided to do a business diploma. After studying two evenings a week for two years I was awarded my diploma with 8 out of 10 distinctions. That got me the Team Leader role in the new department. I had some great managers who constantly supported me.

Don't get me wrong, it was a sacrifice indeed to spend weekends stuck in projects in our home office whilst my husband occupied the children. It was even harder when the sun was out, I could have been with them in the park eating ice cream. It took a lot of will power.

Further managerial roles needed at least degree level or equivalent. At this point, I could have just decided that I had reached my limits. Work was going well - I had just accepted a role managing a team of 6 to deal with new legislation from DfT, (Department for Transport). This role was high profile and hard work, but when my manager put me forward for the Water Professional Diploma HND level at Warwickshire university, I couldn't refuse. Another year of being at university for at least one week a month on top of the full-time job, oh yes, the kids! Having said that, I also couldn't have accepted without the support of my husband and mum.

I ended up being promoted 4 times in 5 years. I felt like I'd found my niche and my understanding of the legislative processes meant I was able to save our company significant financial penalties without going to court. This put me in line for another big promotion, I'll be honest, I wasn't sure I was ready.

I couldn't have done it without my family support, but it was a hard sacrifice it felt at the time. I wanted a better life for my children and I wanted to fulfil a part of my ambition, I was getting the opportunity and I took it.

Lessons learnt:

You must invest in yourself to get to the career path you want.

Sometimes it maybe a sideways step to get the experience.

Think about what the skill or qualification gaps you need to get there.

If you have an aspiration and want to get to the next rung of the ladder, discuss with your line manager.

You may be lucky where your organisation will support you but if not, do it like me.

I took it upon myself to educate myself initially. There are many online courses available now.

What support do you need to achieve your goal?

Do the research and take steps to get it. Don't give up on assumptions that you won't get support.

You really must want to do it!

Get over your self-confidence inhibitions and first knock backs.

If you're not supported where you are, find another path.

Don't think if you did not go down the university route that it's too late! I am proof of that.

5. Building a network

Learning how to use networking as part of my development

In my very early career, I was invited to networking events. In those days it was very much male engineering dominated, full of penguin suits, hardly any women. It would be easy to say no and shy away, but I challenged my very shy self. I loved dressing up and as I was in a junior role, these events felt like a privilege.

These networking events were the start of building my confidence and gaining key allies in the industry. There is much to be said for meeting a stranger, albeit in the same industry and starting up a conversation. I remember a Senior Manager once saying to me, "Rattle your cage! How will you stand out against the crowd if you don't? Get out there!" That really stuck with me.

My role in the water company involved dealing with highway authorities, 32 of them in our patch. I later went on to co-chair the West Midlands Highways and Utilities committee (then the National Highways and Utility conference) and co-chair for DfT centralising performance data, the first in the country. I also became the Communications Director on the National Joint Utilities Group and later Associate Director representing the Tier 1 contractors.

There were many networking opportunities that expanded my knowledge, awareness of new products and innovations working in collaboration with some supply chains that led to awards.

The West Midlands HAUC roadshow was started by some great industry members. As the new Chair, I remember the look of steely eyes from at least 4 male colleagues when I proposed a change to the format by introducing free food and a free industry related seminar by getting more sponsors. It felt like I was stealing their baby, but I wanted success for all of us. We grew the roadshow from 12 exhibitors with 300 people over 2 days to at one time 80 exhibitors and 1200 people over 2 days. Such a success and again had great industry support with a brilliant event manager.

Some of the committee members went on to be my most valued life friends who I learnt so much from.

In my current role I co-chair the people forum and am a member on our women's panel.

There have been many new starters, new apprentices, new graduates over the pandemic where they have had to get used to working online, not getting a chance to be part of the wider organisation culture and maybe developed anxiety from the thought of working from site or office as had to work from home for so long.

I am helping to set up networks and groups that they can join, as it really does help build confidence and meet great industry allies. My last 2 jobs were due to great network contacts putting in a good word for me even though I still had to go through the interview process. It's easier when you are backed by a sponsor who knows you.

Lessons learnt:

Networking opens development, progress and opportunities.

Nervous of crowds? Networking really helps overcome first meet anxiety, it grows you and makes you stronger.

Seize the opportunity don't shy away.

Get involved! Part your knowledge and gain new knowledge.

Bounce ideas for your work to confirm the right action for you and your role within the same industry experts.

Develop a wider colleague circle and use your connections.

Use a networking ally as an external mentor for a different perspective. It has served me well.

Don't forget however, always remain professional at a company /industry related event. You might not get the promotion if you are seen being wheeled away after a drink too many!

6. Managing people

Learning about others

In a way we manage people all the time. Our parents, our siblings, our partners yet when it comes to managing people in a work situation, it can become quite a daunting task because if you're like me, you want to make sure you don't mess it up. You have been trusted and secured a job on the basis you can manage, you want your team to like you.

I was 31 when I first started my role as team leader managing 6. It was daunting and in my early managing days I had a lot to learn.

Looking back, I think I was too mother-like and a bit strict, as I took that role seriously. I wasn't aware of adapting to different personalities, I wasn't aware of my own managerial style either. I suppose I was hard on myself.

The team expanded to 10 then later over 40 but indirectly managing compliance for hundreds in the organisation. With feedback, I became a good people person and I guess I must have done something right, as I'm still in contact with many past employees who all want to stay in touch with me and talk about missing me!

I was very lucky to be included in management development courses in my early career. It was a lightbulb moment when

I learnt about the Myers Briggs Type Indicator. 'People have different styles of personalities and how they want to be managed'.

- Are you an Introvert or Extrovert?

- Are you a Sensing or Intuition type?

- Are you a Thinking or Feeling type?

- Are you a Judging or Perceiving type?

Well so turns out I switch between ISTJ and ESTJ. Lately however, I have built more on my self-confidence and feel I am more of an Extrovert. I'm older and just feel more comfortable with myself.

Together with learning about the 4 colour personalities test, it was a couple of great tools to understand my strengths and development areas as to how I come across to my team and being aware of the different strengths in my team. Everyone is different and every individual has a different key skill set they bring to the table.

I am a big picture, creative, visual get it done type of person. Have too much text on a power point and you have lost me. I do have an eye for detail, but I need an analytical, intuitive member to support me. I also had to learn to stop being so task orientated, have more empathy and time for conversations, be more human!

I got to understand that the more analytical types needed more time to digest what I asked and to reflect and think about the task.

Lessons learnt:

A key learning point for me from a senior manager around difficult performance conversations was to pretend you're talking over a pint in a pub. They don't need to be spoken down to but the coaching, mentoring support can be more effective.

If you become a first line manager, ask for the training and tools to help you manage.

We are all adults, we just need to be spoken to the same way we would like to be spoken to ourself.

Learn to relax and get to know your team members, make time in informal environments. Team build days are great.

I have learnt to listen more as I love doing the talking!

A little praise goes a long way, 'you did a great job', 'thank you' is all it takes.

Every person is an individual, get to know all about them.

Listen, encourage, trust, develop, inspire, help them to be the best version of themselves.

7.

Delivering results

Learning how to bring my experience together

It was 2004 and DfT, Department for Transport announced some major changes to the Utility industry with new legislation. We would have to change as an industry how we plan our jobs to react to emergency and planned jobs for our customers, also understanding the new financial penalties of getting it wrong. This was a major system change and senior management wanted me to be the lead business user.

There was a large legislative document which I was asked to interpret and summarise to our executive board of directors and CEO. Yipes!

I set about by splitting into 3 categories, people, process, systems. It was a lean management tool I had learned.

By interpreting the legislation this way, it really helped my preparation for the board.

If you understand the processes that will change, you can then understand who, from a people point of view will be impacted and therefore what system changes will help with making the process more productive and efficient.

If there are financial penalties attached to key timelines of activity, we need the system to take away as much human intervention as possible.

Picture the scene: I'm having to present to the Executive board, the CEO, and sitting in the audience is my new Senior Manager I had not met beforehand!

I was incredibly nervous but, of course it all went as planned, I had the greatest feedback from a couple of the Directors and my new manager. The CEO was full of praise, saying that my presentation was one of the best he had come across, as it was clear simple and to the point. Even though I had done my preparation and knew my stuff, it was still a real 'pinch myself' moment. Did I really just deliver that?

There was a great project team of 80 at the time. My joint business case with the Project Manager for buying specialist software that dealt with the legislative rules to integrate to the core operational system was accepted also. If anything went wrong, we could run into major financial penalties, it could have delayed the planning of water repair jobs for our customers and a lot more.

Once the project started delivery phase, we needed to track the performance of activity. I was very lucky to be part of a lean management program and learnt some good techniques. To this day it is important that my own department targets are linked to the overall company targets and Key Performance Indicators. It was important my team understood what those objectives were and saw the overall picture so that they felt part of delivering the vision and results.

I held weekly meetings with my team to go through the action tracker to see if we were on track and still adopt the same technique today. It just keeps my team focused and it allows me to give a steer or support if something is falling behind.

We also need to measure our performance, if you can't measure it how do we know if we are improving or not?

As I mentioned in previous chapter, the project was a great success and we went onto win an award. I have applied the same principles in my future jobs.

Lessons learnt:

My mantra is people, process, system. It always works for me, even in my current role, it helped me identify a system need to save time and resource.

If you have the vision, discuss it with the experts to help you achieve it.

Do you ever question the purpose of your role? Is it linked to overall company objectives and KPI's?

Do you ever evaluate the role you are doing and whether it can be improved upon?

Is it productive and efficient? Can It be improved upon by a better process or system?

Can innovation help?

This is where my early factory end to end processes of a manufacturing business together with my business diploma really helped.

If you can visualise everything like a production line, the more repetitive, the more familiar it gets, the speedier and more efficient one gets.

Systems can take over repetitive tasks bringing efficiencies allowing people and the process to be more of a governance, supervision role or free up time to be more productive elsewhere.

Innovation

Learning to trust in change

I have won around 7 awards that I can remember that are work related. I remember what a great feeling it is when you do win, as you have so much pride for the team involved along with the recognition for all the hard work to make it happen.

It's a good way to raise the profile for the cause and those involved, it's a way of sharing best practice for the good of the wider industry.

Innovating and getting buy-in (as innovation often needs funding) can be quite a difficult process in itself. You could be working on a business improvement already and its all about understanding whether a supply chain with a product or service can help as well as any system technologies.

My experiences have taught me two main ways of looking at innovation.

When I was Chair of the WMHAUC roadshow, I was in contact with many of the supply chain so I had good awareness of new products and services on the market by keeping in the loop. As soon as I was made aware of a business process issue that was slowing us down, causing failures or financial penalties I was able to make a link to the right contact.

It is good to have the right contacts, that's where my networking helped. Some ideas need legislation checks or policies to include the innovation and can take some time as acceptance may have to be at various stages of working groups or committees.

Key awards that stand out for me working with colleagues are:

Early trial of intelligent lights to avoid complaints of traffic lights stuck on red and to reduce congestion.

A process whereby sustainable repair material that replaces fossil bitumen after excavation could be made on site in the quantities you needed rather than having to get lorry loads from quarries that can take up valuable time just travelling in the day.

A more recent innovation was working with a subject matter expert on a geographical based mapping tool for compliance governance purposes to avoid serious reputational impacts.

The best experience was delivering the major system project to meet legislation. We worked collaboratively with the supplier when we needed to align and standardise with rest of the market rather than a dated inhouse system.

Lessons learnt:

First, you need to identify a need for innovation.

Will it bring efficiencies or is it a legislative need?

Assess the benefits v cost and whether viable, the business case needs to stack up for senior management buy in and funding.

Arrange demonstrations and live fact finding for the colleagues supporting you.

Understand the stakeholders you need to engage with to get through any legalities or policy change.

Engage with your own colleagues who may be the end user for early feedback.

Ensure the innovation is supported by good processes, good training, and support material.

Communicate, share best practice and then celebrate!

9.

Obstacles or Imposter syndrome

Learning to step out of my own way

Yes, I am BAME in a senior manager role I keep being told and many do ask if I faced any obstacles in my career.

The only one time is when I played Mary in the school nativity play, which I told you about in an earlier chapter. What I didn't mention was that the music teacher didn't think I was the right colour to be Mary, but the drama teacher thought I had the best singing voice so I got to play the lead role anyway. But this has not been the case in my career, no. I have been very lucky.

I was quite surprised to see on the Government website that they updated their guidance since December 2021 and now recommend not to use the term BAME as narrows it down too much. The new term is 'Ethnic Minorities', there is so much more information and it can be difficult to know what the most up to date terminology is, if it keeps changing. I just see us all as one human race and want all to be equals.

On our wonderful cruise, where I had my lightbulb moment, we went to a seminar to learn about the crew and how it works behind the scenes. There are 32 nationalities on that ship and its like one big happy family. I just thought then, whether you are there with your family, friends, members of LGBQT, whatever background, it doesn't matter. You're in the middle of an ocean, regardless of where you are from, in that moment and time you are not in a particular land destination labelled a country, a city or place. You can just be you.

It's the one thing I also like about my current workplace, the culture. We have many colleagues from Europe and feel everyone has respect for each other's cultures, is a place we can learn and celebrate different traditions and festivals.

There is now so much awareness within organisations to help and support women to achieve higher goals and more senior position roles regardless of their background. I can only speak from my own perspective but feel very lucky that I did not meet such obstacles, the only barriers are where my skills did not match the senior position requirements. Perhaps I have held myself back from lack of self-confidence 'imposter syndrome' at times but ask yourself. How many times do you hold yourself back as you are not confident to have the talk with your line manager about a promotion? Have you taken the first knock back as never trying again?

I am not doubting myself anymore. I can honestly say, although I have worked hard for my qualifications later in life, I have had great managers - mostly white, male, middle-aged engineers - who believed in me and gave me a platform. I never felt any obstacles through being an Ethnic Minority. At times I became my own barrier, but I have always had the hunger to be better than I am. The 'eldest child syndrome' will never leave me. As I mentioned, I'm not a celebrity or a top CEO but one has to be satisfied about their own goals in life.

Lessons learnt:

You don't have to be an engineer to work in engineering.

You don't have to feel stuck in the same position.

Young or old, male or female, there are jobs for you in the engineering construction world or any other industry for that matter.

Seize every opportunity and build your network. It will serve you well.

Listen to the positive forces in your life. I thank those in mine. They know who they are.

10. About me

Learning to be myself

So now you know a lot about me. I have been a mother since the age of 21. I have worked full time all my life. My career has been met with great opportunities with some challenges along the way.

I have a great family and am so proud that both of my sons got through university and achieved their degrees, they further went onto do their Masters MSc. Their partners are like the daughters I never had and have the cutest grandson.

I have been healthy all my life, never seen a hospital apart from childbirth. However, my mid-forties were a bit challenging. I had really bad vertigo over 18 months. You don't know it's coming, there are no signs but suddenly you can feel a heat rising to your head, the room is spinning so fast you just have to collapse and get over the nausea feeling. It feels like it is lasting forever but in reality, it's probably a minute or so.

Like my father, I never missed a day of work although it was testing at the best of times. I was very lucky my doctor didn't dismiss it and met a great consultant who diagnosed it down to a rare nerve trigger after many tests and scans. Tablets used for epilepsy treated it within 3 months, fingers crossed it never comes back again.

Soon after, I had a van drive into the back of me whilst I was stationary on the A14 highway in a queue. It made my car go into the car in front of me but due to the type of car I was in, there was little damage. I didn't realise it straight away, but I needed to have steroids in my neck over 2 years as I had a slipped disc.

The children eventually all moved out, we are still very close but it just makes you look at life in a different way. I am seeing myself more as the younger woman, my likes and dislikes. It feels life really took over and everything has passed by in a flash but a time to reflect.

I am a tease, I can be funny, I have a great sense of humour. I always used to play practical jokes until I thought I had better behave and as a manager be a good role model.

I'm a Sagittarian, and I think I really fit the description. I am optimistic, courageous, I love my freedom and independence, I'm honest and very generous, I like to take risks full of fun. However, I don't like those who cross me and am very picky about who I trust. Yes, I am straight to the point and can be quite blunt! Have learnt over time to be softer. When I am angry everyone will know but if I'm hurting, I go into hiding. You may remember, I used to be a performer in my young teenage years, I loved singing, I loved drama, I absolutely love music. I am often to this day caught out humming to myself, my brother-in-law calls me out so many times I don't even know I'm doing it!

Freddie Mercury was my absolute super star; it was so humbling to see his birthplace in Zanzibar. And of course the

Queen song that stood out for me in my younger life was 'I want to break free'.

After he passed away, in the documentary about his life he sings 'Who wants to live forever'. Well, that was it: when I saw that, I really cried and can't even think of that scene without welling up. For the first time I understood every word and realised he sang that knowing he didn't have long to live. This is a lesson I take into my own life - you can't take it with you.

I absolutely love James Bond movies and the theme music titles too, more since Pierce Brosnan became Bond followed by Daniel Craig. The best theme titles for me are by Adele, Skyfall and Sam Smith, Writing's on the wall.

But on a lighter note, as many close to me will know I absolutely love Sean Paul. Certain songs just can't stop me tapping my feet having a jiggle and his songs get me all the time. Ed Sheeran is also one of my other favorite artists, but I like many genres of music and of course I have grown up with bhangra tunes at every wedding reception.

I have been so lucky to travel to many destinations in the world. I love the experience of new cultures, the adventure, the local cuisine, the bars the scenery, exploring the local shops the beaches, the river trips, the desert safari, the hot balloon ride, the helicopter ride. I get a lot of stick about the number of holidays I go on, but like Freddie, I know that you only live once and I am going to live it.

There are much better business authors and books about great strategies. This is about me, my experience and what

I have learnt. If you missed out of an opportunity to gain the right skills or qualifications in your early years, if you have the ambition to better yourself, then go for it! Do it! Make it happen!

I am certainly going to champion this cause and I do hope there is at least one life lesson from me you can relate to or will make you think about doing something different for yourself.

Don't forget to tell me on Instagram @Howigothere2022

Author: Anita Solanki

Anita Solanki is the Head of Interfaces working on a major infrastructure project as part of EKFB. Anita is a second-generation Hindu of Indian heritage and here, she talks about her experiences in the industry and how she has continued learning and growing her network to get to where she is today.

Credits

To my **husband** who has been my rock and let me pursuit my ambitions.

Sarah McKee -a great colleague and friend who inspired me to write my story for a LinkedIn blog in the first place. I am delighted that Sarah could support me to be the editor of my book as she is able to keep the authenticity of my words.

Giuseppe Moschella – Celebrity Apex Cruise Director, the inspiration behind my own book who has provided valuable advice throughout and encouraged me to make it happen as a mentor.

I will be forever grateful for the kindness and support offered to me to achieve my own ambition for this book. Its quite a rare thing that people take out their own time to help someone else amongst their own busy lives.

And to my mum for her support, I dropped out of university but I know I have made you proud.

"Appreciate life, value the little things, respect your friends, treasure the moments, cherish today. Sometimes we forget to thank people after they went the extra mile for us"

Giuseppe Moschella

Printed in Great Britain
by Amazon